DUI:
How To Avoid Arrest!
by Luther Stidham

All Rights Reserved. No part of this publication may be reproduced in any form or by any means, including scanning, photocopying, or otherwise without prior written permission of the copyright holder.

Copyright © 2016 By Luther Stidham

MoFo Books, LLC
Concord, NC
www.MoFoBooks.com

INCLUDES TABLE OF CONTENTS
ISBN 978-0-9863902-2-7

10 9 8 7 6 5 4 3 2

Table of Contents

AUTHOR NOTES 5
About the Author 9
   "Never give up!" 9
A Success Story 11
The Intoxylizer 5000 15
Erratic Driving 17
Implied Consent Offense 27
How It All Works 33
The Enhanced Test 37
The Legal Standard 41
Preparing For The Test 43
Summary 53
Our Pledge 54
Forthcoming Titles: 55
   Prophecy of Justice 55
   Prophecy of Prison 61

AUTHOR NOTES

Let me start by saying that I wrote Falsely Accused Forever Branded, DUI: How to Avoid Arrest!, and the Prophecy of Injustice and Prophecy of Prison series while incarcerated. While all of my subject matters are controversial, they are intended to be informative. I anticipate the release of this book will raise significant questions about the policies and procedures concerning the operation of the Intoxylizer 5000. Perhaps some will argue that I am teaching how to beat its testing method. This is not the case!

    I believe it's only fair to expose how the law allows you or I to be wrongfully convicted of DUI. Here, I expose two secrets behind the Intoxylizer 5000-its minimum legal standard and enhanced testing methods. The "enhanced" testing method will automatically enhance, or raise the suspect's breath alcohol concentration result to a much higher level, and in some instances, nearly double the result.

As a person that went from cop to convict, I firmly believe that I was catapulted into these positions in order to witness horrifying events over the past 11 years. Consequently, I chose to dedicate my life educating the uninformed of their rights to the laws, rules and technicalities of this nation.

With that being said, I assure you, this is only the beginning.

About the Author

"Never give up!"

Luther Stidham, a human rights advocate and author calls himself "the worlds foremost authority on fundamental fairness."

Through his books and interviews, he speaks out against the unfair prejudices and forced pleas in the trial courts, and of the cruel and unusual treatment in our nation's prison system.

Stripped of all opportunity to present any competent defense, Luther served 54 months in prison as a former police officer for a crimes he did not commit. He explored a world he didn't know existed:

"I've learned many things and discovered a broken system."

While serving his sentence, he volunteered his free time as an inmate GED tutor for over 3 years. A handful of inmates now carry their GED Diploma as a result. As a Human Resource Development Assistant Instructor, Luther assisted inmates with constructing their resumes and improving their communication skills, including conducting over 750 mock interviews. He also taught the prison's Computer and Money Smart courses.

A Success Story

As a *jailhouse lawyer*, Luther assisted in writing a Habeas Corpus petition under N.C.G.S. § 17 followed by a Petition for Writ of Mandamus for an inmate housed with him at Gaston Correctional Center in November 2011.

J. Barnette, also known as "R2" had been convicted of a class G felony. However, mistakenly sentenced in the presumptive range for a class F felony, a much higher offense.

By the time R2 met Luther, R2 had already filed a Motion for Appropriate Relief (MAR) sometime in August 2011, to no avail. The Gaston County Superior Court had entered no judgment, and R2 had already completed the sentence for the class G felony.

R2 soon learned of Luther's background in law and sought out his help. Luther was all too happy to help and began working on R2's case right away. Luther filed a *Writ of Hapeas Corpus.*

Now facing sanctions under N.C.G.S. § 17-10, Penalty for Refusal to Grant, which state:

```
If any judge authorized
by this Chapter to grant
writs of habeas corpus
refuses to grant such writ
when legally applied for,
every such judge shall
```

```
forfeit to the party
aggrieved two thousand five
hundred dollars ($2,500),
```

the Honorable Jesse B. Caldwell III, Gaston County Senior Resident Superior Court Judge not only responded within ten days of getting served, but also granted R2's MAR and Habeas Corpus. R2 was released from Gaston Correctional Center on January 5, 2012.

    Due to the mistake in his sentencing hearing, R2's release date was scheduled as far out as April 2012.

    Now at age 42, Luther became inspired by his cell-mates to write about his experience as a police officer and convict. Luther has since dedicated himself to become a human rights advocate and protector of the most abused principle of all — that of fundamental fairness.

The Intoxylizer 5000

The author, a former Boiling Spring Lakes, NC, Police Officer was a person authorized to administer a chemical test utilizing the Intoxylizer 5000, also known in the industry as "I5K". Luther held a permit issued by the Commission for Health Services (now Department of Human Resources) pursuant to G.S. 20-139.1(b)). Neither the author nor MoFo Books, LLC, assumes any liabilities associated with this publication. This is a general overview of the operation of the Intoxylizer 5000. It should be used to achieve understanding of the available testing methods but is not to be relied upon for guidance in a specific application. It is not to be used as a substitute for the opinion or advice of the appropriate legal counsel. To the extent possible, the information is current.

Erratic Driving

We will take a look at the driving characteristics of a drunk driver. Driving in an erratic manner justifies a traffic stop. An officer does not violate the Fourth Amendment by stopping and questioning someone who just committed a traffic violation in the officer's presence. Moreover, routine traffic infractions, even minor ones, provide the reasonable suspicion to stop a vehicle.

Research by the National Highway Transportation Safety Administration (NHTSA) has identified the following indicators of drunk drivers, in descending order of probability that the driver is intoxicated [the percentages indicate the chances out of 100 that a driver exhibiting the behavior is drunk]:

(1) Turning with a wide radius [65%]
(2) Straddling the center or a lane marker [65%]
(3) Appearing to be drunk (gripping the steering wheel tightly, driving with one's face close to the windshield, slouching in the seat, drinking in the vehicle, or staring straight ahead with eyes fixed) [60%]
(4) Almost striking an object or vehicle [60%]
(5) Weaving [60%]
(6) Driving somewhere other than the designated roadway (on the shoulder

or straight through a turn-only lane) [55%]

(7) Swerving [55%]

(8) Slow speed (10 m.p.h. or more below the speed limit) [50%]

(9) Stopping in lane without cause [50%]

(10) Following too closely [50%]

(11) Drifting [50%]

(12) Tires on center or lane marker [45%]

(13) Braking erratically [45%]

(14) Driving into opposing or crossing traffic [45%]

(15) Signaling inconsistent with driving actions [40%]

(16) Stopping inappropriately other than in lane [35%]

(17) Slow response to traffic signals [40%]
(18) Turning abruptly or illegally [35%]
(19) Accelerating or decelerating rapidly [35%]
(20) Headlights off at night [30%]

Of course, if more than one indicator is observed, it is even more likely that the driver is drunk (add 15% to the highest value among the indicators observed). Note that speeding is not an indicator of DUI; because of quicker judgment and reflexes. Once a stop is made, the NHTSA advised that officers should look for the following behaviors:
(1) Difficulty with vehicle controls;
(2) Difficulty exiting vehicle;

(3) Fumbling with license or registration;
(4) Repeating questions or comments;
(5) Swaying, unsteadiness or balance problems;
(6) Leaning on the vehicle (or other objects);
(7) Slurred speech;
(8) Slowness in responding to questions, or asking officer to repeat questions;
(9) Providing incorrect information or changing answers (you have something to hide);
(10) Odor of alcohol.

    In North Carolina and most states across this nation, if you are a suspected of DUI, a certified operator will conduct a chemical analysis of the amount of alcohol in your body. For most, if not all states, anything 0.08 and over and you're legally intoxicated.

First, there are a couple of laws that are important to know, 1) you have the right to call any witness of your choosing to observe you during the test, and 2) you must be observed by the operating officer for at least 30 minutes prior to taking the test. However, once you arrive at an observation area (usually a drunk tank) you must be verbally informed by the operator to the requirement of number 1 above, and the operator has the option of combining both 1) and 2) together.

The 30 minute observation time is to insure that the DUI suspect has not belched during this period. The amount of alcohol vapor emitted after such a belch would interfere with the Intoxylizer 5000's test results. *A belch mandates a restart of the observation time.

Next, in NC, a roadside sobriety test is not mandated by law. The DUI suspect has the right to refuse to participate.

Last, the Intoxylizer 5000 is the only alcohol concentration measuring instrument authorized for use in NC and most other States. The Alco sensor on the other hand is not. It malfunctions and is inaccurate.

Therefore, an officer cannot base a decision to arrest a DUI suspect on the results of the Alco sensor.

However, the NC Court of Appeals ruled in Moore v. Hodges , 116 N.C. App. 727, 449 S.E.2d 218 (1994) "It is permissible to consider the results of Alco sensor test in determining whether trooper had reasonable grounds to *believe* petitioner had committed an implied consent offense."

In this case, the petitioner *consented* to the use of an Alco sensor, therefore, the trooper was allowed to use its results to base a decision to conduct *further* measuring of the petitioner's alcohol by the use of the Intoxylizer 5000.

On the flip side, the Court of Appeals ruled in State v. Ford, 164 N.C. App. 566, 596 S.E.2d 846 (2004); "Alco sensor test results were not admissible in the event of a rehearing on defendant's contempt charge under G.S. 5A-11 because the *results were used to show that defendant was impaired* and that alcohol was the cause of the impairment, and thus the results were inadmissible under G.S. 20-16.3(d). Emphasis added.

I placed emphasis on the above statement because, again, the results of the Alco sensor cannot be used to show a person is impaired, that is, arrest a DWI suspect for a drunk driving based solely on its results.

The DWI suspect can just simply refuse to participate. However, check on your state's laws by contacting an attorney first. This law may have changed since I last wore a badge in 2006.

Implied Consent Offense

Many states have an Implied Consent law similar to North Carolina. In one form or another, the process is the same. North Carolina General Statute § 20-139.1. provides the procedures governing chemical analyses; admissibility; evidentiary provisions, and controlled-drinking programs.

In any implied-consent offense under G.S. 20-16.2, a person's alcohol concentration in the person's body as shown by a chemical analysis is admissible in evidence.

A chemical analysis of the breath administered pursuant to the implied-consent law is admissible in any court if it meets both of the following requirements:

(1) It is performed in accordance with the rules of the Department of Health and Human Services.

(2) The person performing the analysis had, at the time of the analysis, a current permit issued by the Department of Health and Human Services authorizing the person to perform a test of the breath using the type of instrument employed.

   The Department of Health and Human Services shall perform preventive maintenance on breath-testing instruments used for chemical analysis. A court or administrative agency shall take judicial notice of the preventive maintenance records of the Department. However, the results of a chemical analysis of a person's breath performed in accordance with this section are not admissible in evidence if:

(1) The defendant *objects* to the introduction into evidence the results of the chemical analysis of the defendant's breath; <u>*and*</u>

(2) The defendant demonstrates that, with respect to the instrument used to analyze the defendant's breath, preventive maintenance procedures required by the regulations of the Department of Health and Human Services had not been performed

within the time limits prescribed by those regulations.

The methods governing the administration of chemical analyses of the breath shall require the testing of at least duplicate sequential breath samples. The results of the chemical analysis samples are admissible if the test results from any two consecutively collected breath samples do not differ from each other greater than 0.02. Only the lower of the two test results may be used to prove a particular alcohol concentration.

In othe words, two consequtive tests must be given to the defendant and no test result can differ more than 0.02 points.

The Department of Health and Human Services is directed to examine and approve devices suitable for use by law-enforcement officers in making on-the-scene tests of drivers for alcohol concentration. For each alcohol screening device or class of devices approved, the Department must adopt regulations governing the manner of use of the device. For any alcohol screening device that tests the breath of a driver, the Department is directed to specify in its regulations the shortest feasible minimum waiting period that does not produce an unacceptably high number of false positive test results.

How It All Works

When you consume more alcohol than your body can process, your body will expel the excessive alcohol as a vapor through the lungs. Hence, why the breath of someone who has been drinking excessively smells bad. The longer it takes the DUI suspect to be tested the lower the alcohol concentration. We need to be under .08, right?

The I5K begins the test by drawing in fresh air through the mouth piece tubing to insure the testing chamber, a round cylinder, is free from any contaminates, including alcohol molecules. If it's clear, it will produce a 0.00 test result.

    The I5K will then indicate via a display window that it's ready for testing. Once the suspect begins to blow his breath into the tube the I5K will emit a tone. The I5K's display will then indicate a count down of roughly five seconds by displaying several small dots consecutive to each other on the screen. At this point in the test, the I5K will display an asterisk (*) indicating that it has a sufficient amount of the suspect's breath for a proper chemical analysis. The latter of the two tests generally takes less than six seconds.

Alcohol molecules are distinctive and are only detected and measured inside the testing chamber. The I5K will then display the results of the suspect's alcohol concentration. A confirmatory test is required for final analysis.

The Enhanced Test

Most DUI suspects are told by the I5K operator to begin the test by saying something similar to "I want you to start blowing as hard as you can, as long as you can and don't stop until I tell you to." Sound familiar? Here's why.

When a person completely exhales, there's a small amount of air left over in your lungs that can only be expelled by squeezing your chest muscle tightly. That small amount of air is called "deep air content." That little amount of air holds the highest alcohol concentration.

Although the I5K will indicate by the asterisk that it has obtained enough of the suspect's breath to properly (and legally) analyze, it will *not* begin measuring the alcohol concentration until the defendant *stops* blowing. Therefore, when the operator instructs the suspect to blow as hard as he can and not to stop until instructed, it is only to get to the deep air content, which will automatically enhance, or raise the suspect's breath alcohol concentration result to a much higher level, and in some instances, ***nearly*** DOUBLE the result.

For example, during my I5K certification training, we were instructed how to be aggressive enough to get to the DUI suspect's deep air content.

Each officer had to be assigned a designated driver and we each consumed a sufficient amount of alcohol for one hour. I'm not a big drinker, so I consumed four bottles of a lemonade based alcohol beverage.

In utilizing the "enhanced" testing method during the first test, the I5K revealed that my alcohol concentration was **0.10**.

Pay attention here!

In North Carolina, I was considered legally intoxicated. However, after retesting using the "legal standard" testing method my result dropped to **0.06**.

Two points below North Carolina's legal limit.

"WOW!" I thought.

The Legal Standard

To begin the test, air from the lungs must be blown into the breath tube.

First, the I5K *will then* indicate via a tone that it has detected enough pressure emitted by my lungs.

Second, after a brief amount of time, it will then display the asterisk indicating that it has enough of my breath to legally analyze for the amount of alcohol concentration in my system.

Anything more is not necessary and only designed to produce a higher test result.

Preparing For The Test

Time, belching and deep breaths are our friends here, and all work together. Without one, you restrict the end result. As a former permit carrying breathanalizer, this is what I would do.

First, in North Carolina, I would refuse to take *any* field sobriety test. Unless the law has changed or changes, this is not required, so I cannot be charged with the refusal. To be sure, I would ask specifically "Does the law require that I participate?" If I get any other answer than "yes," the answer is "NO."

Second, since most patrol vehicles have cameras and the officers are wearing wireless mics, I would say as little as possible and stay in my vehicle. I am only required to answer questions pertaining to my identification. For example, if the officer asked "how much have you had to drink?" My answer would be "I'm invoking my *Miranda* Rights," followed up with the silent treatment.

    Next, unless the officer has verbally told me that I am under arrest, I am not required by law to exit my vehicle unless my vehicle is in the way of traffic. So I would be very cautious to pull far enough off the highway to be out of harms way. If unsure, I would say,

"I feel my safety is better served within the confinement of my vehicle."

Depending upon the officer's response, I would then follow up with asking, "am I breaking any laws by staying in my vehicle?"

If asked by the officer, I am required to provide my drivers license, registration and proof of insurance. That's it. Remember this, if I am in any type of traffic stop, even for something simple, say, no seat belt, I am being detained. I am in a form of temporary custody because I cannot just up and leave when I want to. I have a right to REMAIN SILENT!!!!

Third, on the ride to the police station, and while in the drunk tank, I would very *discretely* take long deep breaths. Slowly inhale deep then exhale; then exhale more. Meaning, forcing out every last drop of air in my lungs by tightening the chest muscles.

This action removes the "deep air content" from the lungs, which is the most important part. This will insure that I inhale fresh air. If the police officer inquires what I'm doing or something similar, again, I wouldn't speak, I cannot be charged for not speaking.

If I were to accidentally belch, by protocol this mandates my 30 minute observance time to start over. But as a reminder, I need to be very careful here because I could be charged with tampering with the test. However, the burden of proof is on the officer.

By law, I am only required to blow hard enough to activate the tone and I can stop when the display window indicates with the asterisk. For example, I am not required to "blow as hard as I can", this is a trick.

The solution?

I would take a very deep, deep, deep breath and begin blowing *just* hard enough to activate the tone, then hold that pressure steady.

The display window would look something similar to this example (* . . . .). The dots will display from right to left, one-by-one followed by the asterisk.

If I blow into the tube as hard as I can, I will run out of air quick and be forced to use my "deep air content." As you'll recall, not a goof idea.

As I'm blowing air into the tube, I would watch the display window, if it's positioned so that I cannot see the display, I would reposition myself to view it. If the operator refused to allow me to watch the display I would inform him that I have a right to insure that he or she is not using the enhanced testing method.

The instant the I5K displayed the asterisk, I would stop blowing. Anything more and I would only be hurting myself. Nowhere is it written in North Carolina's Statutes that I must continue any further than the minimum legal standard. Again, if the officer gets argumentative about me watching the display window, I would remind him or her that I have a constitutional right to insure that the enhanced testing method was not being used. This is where a good witness comes in. If I can't watch the window, my witness can.

As a last resort, I would demand a blood test to be performed by a certified person, usually a registered nurse.

At trial, I would object to the admission of its results based on the fact that *the Department of Human Services failed to perform the required maintenance as scheduled.* I would then ask the state to produce evidence sufficient to prove the trier of fact that the instrument was, in fact, maintained on schedule by the Department.

If all else failed, I would plead not guilty at trial and state on record that I was denied the opportunity to insure that only the minimum legal standard was used. If the operator used the enhanced testing method instead, I would also state, again, on record, the following language:

"I object to the admission of the test result on the ground that the operator used enhanced testing methods designed to produce a result greater than that of the legal limit."

The best way, and in my opinion, the only way to have a true alcohol chemical analysis is to have a blood test.

Summary

Let me stress that the information I have shared is not to be used or taken as legal advise. Always consult with an attorney.

Well, I hope that you find this book informative. I also hope that you never drink and drive, and besides, it's illegal and dangerous.

Visit my website often at MoFoBooks.com for more information and to stay up-to-date on my forthcoming titles.

Good luck.

Our Pledge

MoFo Books and the author, Luther Stidham are dedicated to protecting the most protected principle of all — that of fundamental fairness. The laws, rules, and technicalities in this country should apply to use all, both great and small. The size of a man's bank account should not determine the outcome of his trial. Our judicial officials, and bar members should not stoop to such underhanded schemes to secure a conviction.

    In the end, we are all equal.

Forthcoming Titles:

Prophecy of Justice

Prophecy of Justice, is based on a true story drawn from a dozen interviews and hundreds of pages of documents.

The scenes described in this book were re-created, based on the information discovered within several documents, and from my own recollection of events that I have related to the best of my knowledge. I recognize that my memories of the events described in this book may differ from those of the people characterized here. This book is not intended to hurt or embarrass any of the individuals I portray. I am sure they are each fine, decent, and hard-working people who, in my opinion, made poor choices that ultimately led to my wrongful incarceration.

With a few exceptions, I have tried to keep the chronology as close to exact as I possibly could. In some instances, details and descriptions have been changed or recreated to coincide with the documentary record.

Except for the few individuals in the public eye, the names and personal descriptions of the people populating this story have been altered to protect their privacy. The dialogue has been re-created, based on the recollections of the participants and the actual case file documents.

This book will carry a high level of interest because of how it could affect the public's trust and opinion of our justice system.

Ask yourself these simple questions: What does the public expect from the criminal justice system? How does the public perceive various components of the criminal justice system? Is the system considered fair?

Finally, and most important: How much of public opinion is rooted in individual opinion, and in personal experiences?

You are the public; so am I.

I believe my personal story will reflect what factors currently affect public confidence and will reveal what has been learned about the way public confidence in the criminal justice system is built.

My story is a cut-away and cross section of a brutal, severely-broken justice system. In the writing of this personal memoir, I have come to a level of understanding that makes it undeniably obvious that I am *not* alone. Others like me are mere trade-offs. We were bartered in exchange for a prosecutor's misguided, personal agenda.

I have come to another level of understanding that makes it

undeniably clear that my story stands as a living example that *all* suspects are judicially presumed guilty until proven innocent, to one degree or another; and that all men are created equal, just not equally entitled to judicial protection by our laws, rules, and legal technicalities. The size of a man's bank account should not determine the quality of his defense options and prospects, nor the quality of his prosecutorial offense.

  Like an investment, the judicial tag-team members brand their suspect through the media with a pre-trial guilty verdict as the payoff in the court of public opinion.

In my personal story, you are the jury.

While I have a surrogate doing the work for you, it is *you* who must ultimately sift through the information, and it is you who will be left thunderstruck and boiling with rage by what you discover.

Prophecy of Prison

Prophecy of Prison, is a dramatic and realistic portrayal of events during my incarceration of the battles I faced with the Brunswick County Superior Court Division and the Attorney General's office. I re-created the scenes in this book based on the information contained from several documents, interviews, and from my own recollection as to what occurred.

The lies and corruption followed me to prison. Because my case was so close to that of the Duke Lacrosse scandal, I expected help from this state's highest attorney, Roy

Copper. I quickly learned that his pack of wolves stood waiting to devour me. The documents and evidence I presented in *Prophecy of Justice* were sent certified mail to his office. He, like my attorney, gave no response. It was then that it became clear; his only goal was to keep the incarcerated — incarcerated, at all cost.

By the end of *Prophecy of Prison*, I was still deeply effected by my conviction. What I expected to be a life of law enforcement had become a traumatic, soul-wrenching experience.

My wife, Danette, born and raised in Charlotte, was proud that her husband had finally settled in a career. Our son, Nathan, and my two other boys, Jesse and Jordan, were also proud of their father and looked to me for guidance.

We lived a comfortable life. For the first time, we had built our first house by the blood and sweat of our own hands, and it meant everything to use. My wife and children drove countless nails right there beside me. We were living the American dream.

But how had it all begun? What had shaped my mind and my life? What had led to the broken dream and to my frantic fight as a convict to fit in?

It wasn't any one incident, of course, but a series of subtle influences and events that swept me along.

While I'm not finished with the first world, in the *Prophecy of Prison*, I'm writing about the second world — *the repressive prison profiteers*. The TV shows about prison are not what they seem. You're not allowed to see what goes on behind scenes. You're led to believe the convict is a vile diseased rodent, worthy of nothing, and the guards are upstanding law abiding citizens. That they obey the rules, policies and procedures of the state's prison system. I can tell you first hand, we all have been mislead.

What you, the tax paying public should know is what truly goes on behind these walls. This environment is all things short of rehabilitation. It's a horrifying brewing ground for torture, brainwashing, and hostility. From the administration personnel to the guards, *most* are abusive, arrogant, conceited, insolent, narcissistic, ostentatious, presumptuous Hitler portraying tyrants. Oh, and did I mention—they are also sadistic liars? This is especially true for the inmate's case manager.

But I was glad to have met them because I know that they would be a part of my past. They will no longer be part of my life. They are like a sore that had been healed and could no longer threaten me.

I survived physically, not because I was tougher or better than those around me, but because, by the grace of God, he wanted me to. Through me, he had purpose.

Throughout the *Prophecy of Prison*, besides my own discoveries and battles, my wife and co-author Danette, has shared her own memories. We both have shared our most intimate letters from each other while I was behind bars. And in addition, I decided—for better or worse—to share stories from the other inmates.

Periodically, I write about the laws, rules, and technicalities of this state and country. I do my best to interpret them from my own understanding for the uninformed. I don't give any legal advise, and this book is not to be intended to be taken for legal advise. Always consult with a good attorney.

You may also notice that I never call the guards by their, technically, official state position title—*Correctional Officer*. In my books, or rather belief, an *officer* is a symbol of honor. A title earned by passing a 600 plus hour basic law enforcement training course. Or even a rank you earn in this great country's courageous military. Unlike the North Carolina Division of Prison, now referred to as the Department of Public Safety, you don't instantly become an *officer* simply by strapping on a gun and pinning on a badge on yourself. They are not *officers*. And I ask you, the reader, as a favor to me, never call a Department of Public Safety prison guard an *"officer,"* especially if they are employed at Gaston Correctional Center. Most prison guards that I've met don't have the dignity to be called, *"officer."* They're prison guards, and that's all.

    I once read somewhere that Paul Harvey said something like "if you want to meet some of the lowest scum on earth? Visit any prison USA. The trick is, you have to be at the prison gate at shift change."

-Luther Stidham

www.ingramcontent.com/pod-product-compliance
Lightning Source LLC
Chambersburg PA
CBHW050607300426
44112CB00013B/2107